For Megan
C. S.
For Rafael and Emile
J. V.

Text copyright © 2017 by Claire Saxby
Illustrations copyright © 2017 by Julie Vivas

First U.S. edition 2017

Library of Congress Catalog Card
Number pending
ISBN 978-0-7636-9481-4

17 18 19 20 21 22 LEO 10 9 8 7 6 5 4 3 2 1

Printed in Heshan, Guangdong, China

This book was typeset in Adobe Garamond
and Berliner Grotesk.
The illustrations were done in watercolor.

Candlewick Press
99 Dover Street
Somerville, Massachusetts 02144

visit us at www.candlewick.com

Koala

CLAIRE SAXBY

illustrated by **JULIE VIVAS**

CANDLEWICK PRESS

In a high tree fork, a gray ball unfurls. Tall as a toddler, a sleepy young koala sniffs at leaves. His nose is dark and leathery. His soft ears twitch, and his brown eyes blink. He has two extra thumbs, and paws perfect for climbing.

Climb, little Koala.
It's dinnertime.

Koalas eat the leaves of only a few of the many types of eucalyptus trees. These leaves are poisonous to most animals.

Koala is thirsty and nuzzles
at his mother's pouch.
But for the first time, Koala
cannot make his way in.

8

When he tries again,
his mother swats him away.

Koalas are marsupials and
suckle their young in a pouch.
Baby koalas are called joeys.

He climbs beyond her reach,
takes a mouthful of leaves,
and chews slowly.

Climb, little Koala.
It's time to find your own way.

Once a koala is pregnant again,
she will ignore her joey. Young koalas
must look after themselves from then
on, though they may stay close by for
another year.

11

In the night, Koala startles from his sleep-curl as a roar tears the air. It is louder than a snoring grandfather, closer than thunder. In his waking panic, Koala reaches for his mother. But she is not there.

The thundering koala, another male,
pushes at him.
Koala tumble-climbs to the ground.
He scrambles back to his home tree,
but before he can reach the first branches,
the male rumbles again.

Move on, little Koala.
Find a new home.

From late spring to the end of summer, male koalas
search for mates. They fight any other male koalas they meet.
These fights are always noisy and can be violent.

Koala retreats, uncertain
and unsafe on the ground.
He listens to earth sounds,
then sniffs at the base of a
large eucalypt. The bark stinks.
It is a warning—stay away!

Mature male koalas have a scent
gland on their chest. They rub
against the bark at the base
of a tree to claim it as their own.

16

Koala has never
been to this part
of the forest before.
He searches
and listens,
sniffs and hesitates.
Koala climbs, but
the bark is loose,
and he falls.

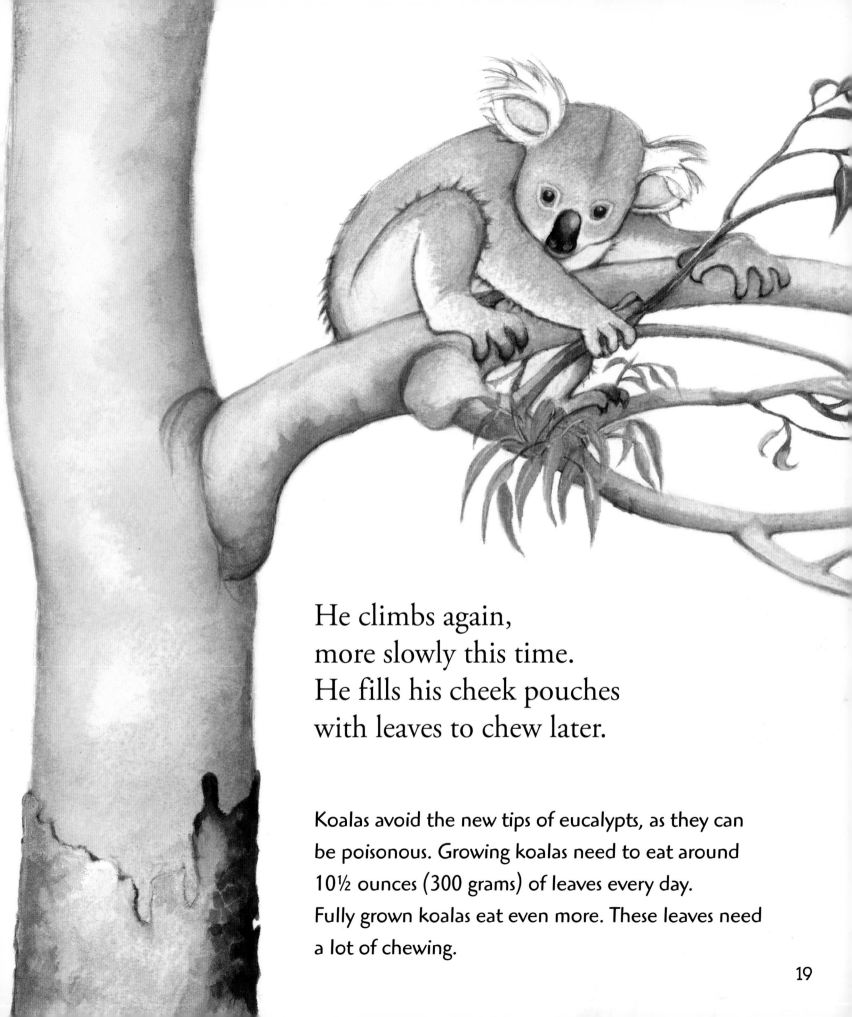

He climbs again,
more slowly this time.
He fills his cheek pouches
with leaves to chew later.

Koalas avoid the new tips of eucalypts, as they can
be poisonous. Growing koalas need to eat around
10½ ounces (300 grams) of leaves every day.
Fully grown koalas eat even more. These leaves need
a lot of chewing.

Koala travels farther and farther
from his mother. He eats when he can
and sleeps where he can.

Move on, little Koala.
Find a new home.

Several koalas may share the same forest
but will seldom share a tree. Koalas mostly
live alone except when seeking a mate.

One wild night,
the wind grows until even
the tallest tree sways like a sapling.
Koala clings tight,
safe and warm as raindrops
plomp and plit around him.

Koalas can sleep through even fierce storms.
Their thick, oily fur acts like a rain jacket, keeping
them dry even in heavy rain.

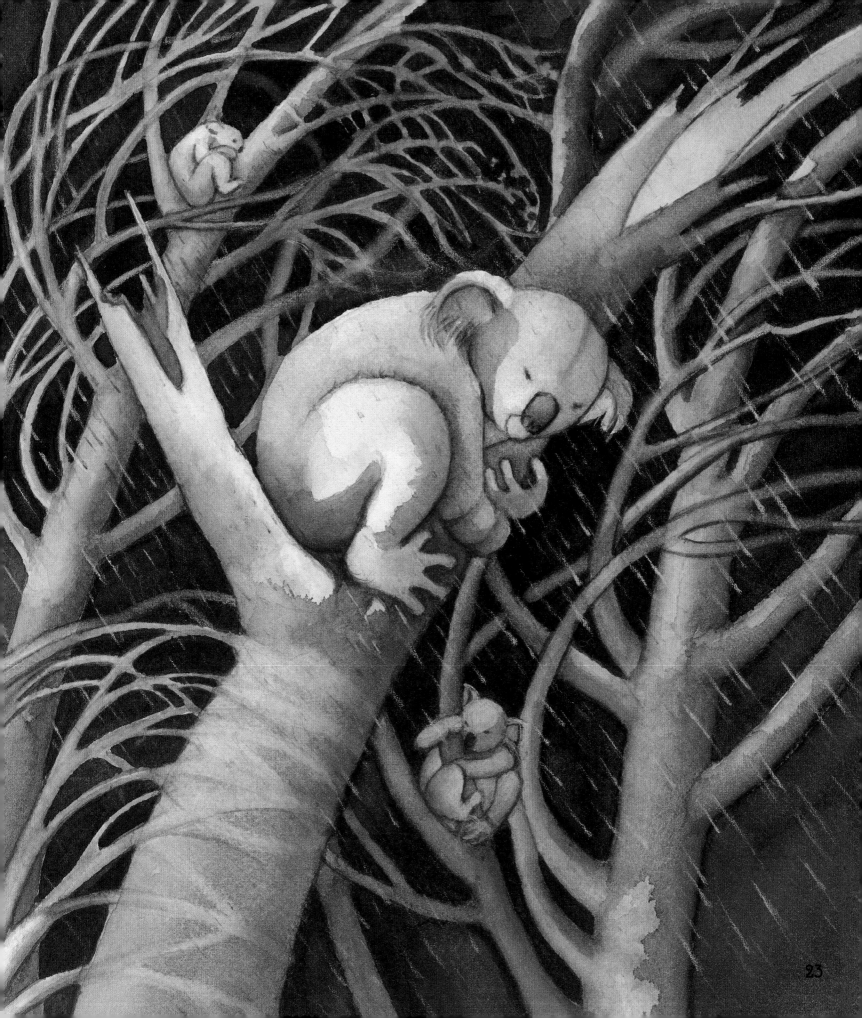

It is dawn before the storm is done.
In the pale morning, Koala spies a
large stand of trees beyond a clearing.
As he touches the ground, a snake
uncoils in the leaf litter.
Koala startles and launches himself
across the clearing, reaching with
his front paws, jumping with his
hind legs.

Faster, little Koala, faster.

When koalas move slowly, they use all four
limbs in turn, but if they are in a hurry, they hop
with their hind legs together, like kangaroos.

25

Only when he is far above
the ground does Koala stop
and look around.
He sees other koalas,
but they are not too close.
Koala eats until he is full.
A breeze gentles his fur,
and he shifts.

Stay, little Koala.

This will be a good home.

Koalas are found only in Australia. They are marsupials, or pouched mammals, and live in trees. They can sleep up to eighteen hours a day. Their waking time is spent eating and grooming. In northern Australia, male koalas weigh up to 20 pounds (9 kilograms) and have light-gray coats. Koalas in the south have darker coats and are larger, with males weighing up to 30 pounds (14 kilograms). In both the north and south, females are smaller than males. Koalas generally remain in a small home range. Females may stay in the same small area for their lifetime, moving only if they run out of food. Males may have to roam farther in search of a mate.

INDEX

Look up the pages to find out all about these koala things.

Don't forget to look at both kinds of words –

this kind and **this kind.**